X

Making a Miniature Theatre

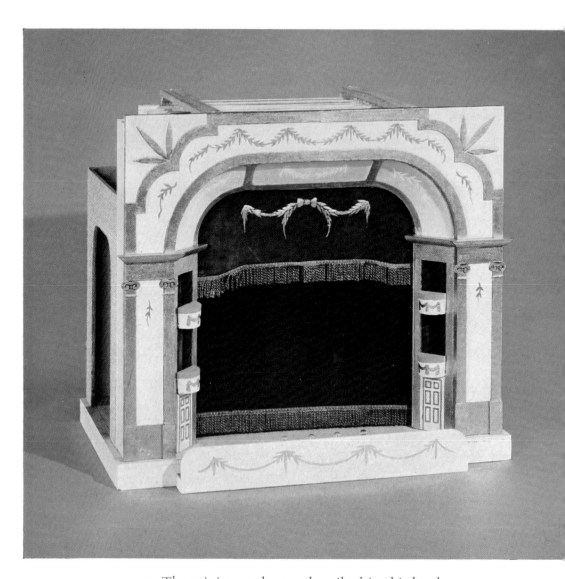

1. The miniature theatre described in this book

Making
a Miniature Theatre

GUY R. WILLIAMS

Publishers
P L A Y S , I N C
Boston

First American edition published by
Plays, Inc. 1967

Printed in Great Britain

This book is dedicated
to all the young people
who have first experienced
the magic of the theatre
on the stage at Parmiter's School

Contents

Plates

Introduction

We all enjoy a visit to the theatre. From the moment when we first take our seats in the auditorium and look round at the people who are preparing to enjoy the entertainment with us, to the final blackout or fall of the curtain we will find ourselves in an extraordinary world where colours tend to be brighter, movements more graceful, amusing situations funnier, and crises more dramatic than they are in our normal day-by-day life.

Are you lucky enough to be able to go to the theatre often? Or is a visit to a play, or to the opera, or to a ballet a rare treat, to be looked forward to for weeks and remembered afterwards with pleasure and gratitude? Even if you have been to a real theatre only once in your lifetime, you will know that a glimpse of a well-lit colourful stage can be an unforgettable experience. That is why so many grown-up people, offered a treat, will choose an evening at the playhouse in preference to any other kind of amusement. There is a magic about the theatre that is quite unlike all other forms of enchantment.

Fortunately, anyone who likes model-making can capture at home some if not all of the exciting atmosphere of the theatre by making a miniature stage. No special skills are called for, and the project need not be expensive. In this book, you will find instructions for making the miniature theatre shown on the cover. It can be a source of great pleasure to own such a theatre, and to be able to design suitable scenery for it, and to arrange miniature lighting in it. You should be able to complete the proscenium and a few simple settings in less time than it would take you to rehearse and stage a real, full-length theatrical production.

1

How it All Started

First, you may like to know what a proscenium is, and how the "picture stage" (as opposed to the open stage and the arena stage) developed. You can skip this chapter altogether if you are eager to start collecting your equipment and finding your materials.

THE ORIGINS OF THE THEATRE. As far as we can tell, the first "theatrical performances" of any kind took place many centuries before men knew how to make permanent buildings for any specific purpose. These meetings were intended to propitiate the gods, to produce rain, or to bring success to the hunters of a primitive community. Probably, there would be an assembly of excited people in some well-trodden place, and the items on the programme would be more like a series of ritual dances than the dramas and comedies we associate with the theatre today. Some of the meetings may well have culminated in sacrifices of various kinds.

GREEK THEATRES. The next great step in the development of theatres came when the Greeks discovered certain places that were especially suitable for their important gatherings—they chose natural hollows in convenient hillsides so that as many people as possible could see and hear what was going on. The members of the audience sat in tiers on the grassy slopes and looked down on the performers, who used a circular flat area of ground called the "orchestra".

By the fourth century B.C., many of these hollows had been further developed. In some, the ground had been excavated so that each tier of seats could form part of the circumference of a circle. Stone slabs made the seating permanent (if not particularly comfortable), and a simple building or *skene* was provided

13

behind the orchestra so that the performers could retire from view when they wanted to change their costumes or masks.

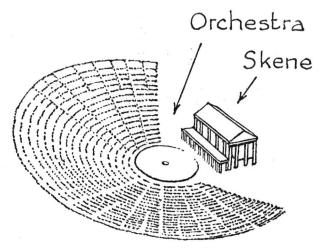

1. *This is how a Greek theatre may have been arranged*

ROMAN THEATRES. The Romans were great borrowers of other people's ideas, and they built theatres that resembled in many respects the theatres of the Greeks. Usually, though, Roman theatres were a little smaller than Greek theatres, possibly because they were actual buildings and not just sloping tracts of ground.

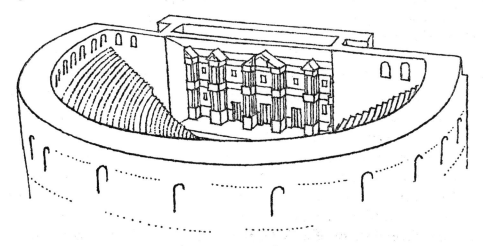

2. *A partial reconstruction of a Roman theatre*

Each Roman theatre that has survived seems to have had a semi-circular orchestra, a raised stage, and a sumptuously decorated *frons scaenae* at the back of the stage, with three doors at least for the actors and actresses to pass through. Unlike Greek theatres, Roman playhouses were partly roofed or sheltered by awnings, so that the weather, good or bad, should not interfere with the performances.

THE MEDIEVAL THEATRE. In north-west Europe, in the Middle Ages, miracle plays and pageants were presented under less formal conditions, but with immense vigour and enjoyment, usually under the auspices of the priests, and generally in the precincts of a church.

Later, as their popular appeal increased, many of these performances took place on wheeled platforms, or "pageant wagons", which could be moved about to the various parts of a town. At York and Chester, and maybe at other places, the different scenes which made up the action of one of these spectacles would each be allotted a separate wagon. Then, the whole story could be told by changing the positions of the wagons.

3. *This shows the possible shape of a medieval pageant wagon*

Away from these great centres of dramatic activity, rustic audiences relied for their entertainment on the efforts of small troupes of travelling players. These wanderers made use of rough platforms set up in the yards of inns, in the halls of the great houses, and occasionally, when the actors were especially favoured, in the royal palaces. There were no permanent public playhouses in England until the reign of Queen Elizabeth I. Then, round and many-sided buildings like the famous "Globe" were put up to satisfy the growing demand for drama.

4. *Theatres in the reign of Elizabeth I and James I may have looked something like this. The lower drawing shows part of the interior*

RENAISSANCE PLAYHOUSES. Meanwhile, in Italy, theatres were being erected which were not unlike the architecturally impressive buildings that had survived, at least in part, from classical times. One of the most important of these Renaissance playhouses was the Teatro Olimpico that was designed by Andrea Palladio, at Vicenza. In it, the formal background to the stage was broken by three enlarged doorways, through each of which a convincing perspective view of a street could be seen. This innovation was to have a profound influence on theatre design, and we may see in it the origins of the picture-frame stage in which a strong proscenium arch acts as a useful support for movable scenery.

THEATRES IN THE PAST THREE CENTURIES. From that time until quite recently, the picture-frame stage, with or without an "apron" (that is, part of the stage which projects forward into the auditorium) has been regarded as a normal and inevitable feature of all European theatres and opera houses. Now, experiments are being made with arena stages, semi-arena stages, and other less traditional acting spaces. These may be dramatically very effective, leading as they do to a great sense of intimacy between the actors and actresses and their audience, but they do not appeal to the model-maker quite as strongly as theatres of a more conventional type.

The miniature theatre shown on the cover may seem a little old-fashioned if you are used to advanced drama, but it is quite compact, and you can add any extensions you like to your model to make it up to date or even *avant-garde*. The best models, after all, are those that reflect truthfully the likes and dislikes of the people who have made them.

SUMMING UP. Various as they may be, all the kinds of theatre mentioned in this chapter have one very important feature in common—they are places where the performers and their audiences are in direct contact with each other, where the performances are, in the fullest sense of the word, "alive". This gives them a quality that is inevitably missing from film and television shows, however excellent technically these may be. The theatre's most potent enchantments cannot be canned.

2

Making a Miniature Theatre

Before you start work in earnest on your theatre, look round your home and choose some small part of it to be your temporary workshop. You will need:

A firm surface to work on. A work bench would be ideal. If you have to use one of your domestic tables, put an old blanket over it, or a sheet of hardboard, or several sheets of newspaper, so that you will not scratch or stain it accidentally. *Shelf space or cupboard space.* For storing the components of your theatre as you make and assemble them.

Boxes. Cardboard, wood or plastic, to hold the small bits and pieces that can so easily get lost.

You will not need a lot of space—model theatre building is almost a fireside hobby —but it does help to have a small area that you don't have to tidy every time a meal is served.

A VICE. It is not very easy to make anything with wood unless you have some means of holding the pieces securely while you work on them. A carpenter's vice is specially designed for this. If you have no vice you can improvise by clamping the components tightly to a table top.

THE TOOLS YOU WILL NEED. Fortunately, you will not have to spend a lot of money on tools and equipment—in fact, you will probably find most of the items listed below in your home (or garage) already.

A saw. A tenon saw will be large enough. For cutting plywood, you will find a panel saw useful. This is a cross-cut saw with very fine teeth.

A wheel brace. For drilling holes. You will need a small selection of Morse pattern drills to use with it.

A screwdriver, or, better, two of different sizes—one for small screws, say to size 6, and one for larger screws.

A chisel. For chopping out and making joints. A bench chisel with a blade about ¾ in. wide will be generally useful.

A hammer, with nails and panel pins. You may be able to do without these altogether.

A steel plane or Jack plane for smoothing the outside edges of the components. This too is optional. You can use a Surform tool instead, or glasspaper (Middle 2 Grade, followed by Grade No. 1).

When you start to decorate your theatre and to make scenery for it, you will need a pair of scissors, a sharp penknife, and a pair of pliers, and you may find a bradawl useful for making small holes.

ADHESIVES. For joining wood to wood, you can use Scotch glue, the traditional adhesive that has to be heated in a double pot (glue, with a little water, in the inside container; water alone in the outer jacket).

Less bother, and just as effective, are the modern synthetic glues such as "Aerolite" and "Casco Glue-All", or the excellent impact or contact glues, such as "Evo-Stik".

For sticking paper to paper, or paper to card, use a ready-mixed paste like "Gloy" or one of the adhesives made by stirring a quick-dissolving powder with cold water.

DRAWING. For marking out work accurately, use an HB or H pencil, a rule with a straight edge, and a set square—or a carpenters' try square, if you have one. A darker pencil such as a B or 2B will be more suitable for rough sketch designs. A soft india-rubber will be useful.

OILSTONES AND STROPS. For keeping your edged tools sharp, you will need an oilstone, either natural or artificial, of a medium grade. You can make a strop by gluing a piece of leather to a piece of wood. It will be convenient if one end of the latter can be shaped to act as a handle.

Leather → Wood

5. An easily made strop

MATERIALS. Use wood for the main components of your miniature theatre, as it is easily worked, pleasant to touch, and will stand up to a considerable amount of heavy handling.

The base can be made of a good quality well-seasoned hardwood if this is available, as this will provide a sound and inert foundation for the whole model. Blockboard, ½ in. or 1 in. thick, is cheaper, and quite as satisfactory. Good quality plywood can also be recommended, and this should certainly be used for all the "sheet" parts that are to make up the proscenium arch and the stage surround, except the front arch, Part B. Each part will be described in more detail in Chapter 3, but if you happen to live in a district where plywood has to be ordered in advance you may find the diagram given in Illustration 6 helpful at this point—it shows how one sheet of 5 ply, 4 ft. × 4 ft., can be divided to

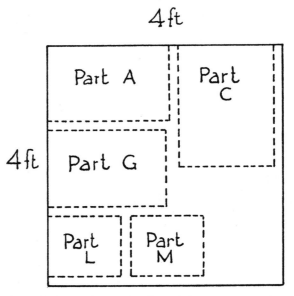

6. One sheet of plywood provides five of the six principal components of the miniature theatre

provide five of the six largest components. A piece of blockboard 24 in. ×
20 in. × ½ in. provides the sixth sheet.

Soft woods, such as white pine, and stripwoods such as spruce or obeche
(which can be obtained from any shop that supplies materials for hobbies and
handicrafts) can be recommended for the few remaining structural members.

TECHNICAL NOTES

Here are brief descriptions of some of the simple operations you will have to
carry out when you are building the main structure of your miniature theatre.
If you are an experienced woodworker already, you will not need to refer to
them.

CUTTING WOOD EXACTLY TO SIZE. When you want to finish any wood component to an exact size, begin by producing one perfectly flat side as a 'datum'
from which to work.

Then plane (or rub down) one of the adjoining edges so that the edge is perfectly flat, too, and so that it is exactly at right angles to the face side. Use a try
square, if you have one, to check the accuracy of this.

Then mark the prepared face and edge so that you will readily recognize
them (Illustration 7).

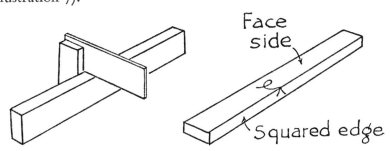

7. *A try square is used* (left) *for checking right angles. A bench
mark is used* (right) *for identifying the first finished surfaces*

With these two surfaces from which to take measurements, you should find
it fairly easy to plane or rub down the piece of wood so that it is the required
width and thickness. When you are sawing it to the required length, make it a

little oversize, and then plane it or rub it down to the exact dimension with a final trim.

HOW TO USE A SAW. Illustration 8 shows how a handsaw should be held—with the forefinger pointing along the line of the blade. You can use the thumb of your left hand to guide the saw blade when you are starting a cut. Make the cut or "kerf" on the waste side of a measured line.

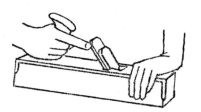

8. *The correct way to hold a handsaw*   9. *The correct way to hold a plane*

HOW TO USE A PLANE. If you are going to use a plane, you will get the best results if you hold it in the traditional way. Grip the handle with your right hand, so that your forefinger can rest on the end of the cutter. Your left hand, at the front of the plane, will help to control its direction (Illustration 9).

Illustration 10 shows the best way to apply pressure to a plane—at the front of the tool with your left hand at the beginning of each stroke: at the back of the tool with your right hand at the end of each stroke.

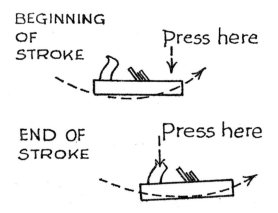

10. *This shows how downward pressure should be applied when a plane is being used*

How to sharpen a penknife. Put a few drops of neats' foot oil or cycle lubricating oil on your oilstone. Then hold the blade of the knife with both your hands, as shown in Illustration 11, and rub the cutting edge backwards and forwards. Do this for both sides of the blade, then finish by drawing the blade gently backwards on the leather strop.

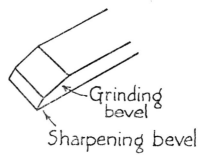

11. *Hold a penknife like this while you sharpen its blade*

12. *These two bevels are needed on a chisel*

How to sharpen a chisel. When you buy a chisel you will find that it already has one bevel, known as the "grinding bevel", at an angle of 20° or 25°. Before you can use the chisel, you will have to make a second bevel, or "sharpening bevel" at an angle of 30° or 35° (Illustration 12 shows both bevels).

First, put the chisel with the grinding bevel flat on the oilstone. The blade will be raised at an angle of 20° or 25°.

Then raise the chisel so that it is at an angle of 30° or 35°, and move it backwards and forwards until the cutting edge develops a small burr or "wire edge". To remove this, put the chisel flat on the oilstone with the bevelled side upward and then move the tool gently backwards and forwards. Then finish by stropping the cutting edge gently on your piece of leather.

How to sharpen a plane blade. To remove the cutting iron from a metal plane—if you have one—you will have to release the lever cap.

To remove the cutting iron from a wooden jack plane or trying plane, put the back end of the plane against your thigh, and then strike the button on the front of the plane. This will provide a gentle pivotting movement that will release the wedge which is keeping the iron in place.

When sharpening the iron, hold it with its bevel flat against the oilstone (as in Illustration 13), raise the end slightly to make a second bevel, and work it backwards and forwards. If you give a little extra pressure with your right hand and your left hand alternately, the cutting edge will be slightly curved, which is desirable.

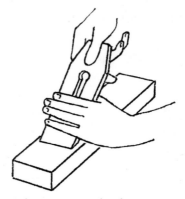

13. *Sharpening a plane's cutting iron*

Check from time to time to see that there are no gaps or gashes in the cutting edge. If you are using the oilstone correctly, you should eventually raise a distinct burr. Then put the iron flat side down on the oilstone, and move it backwards and forwards once or twice. This will turn the wire edge to the bevel side. Reverse the iron and repeat the process until the wire edge breaks away, or, if you prefer, strop the edge of the cutter on the palm of your hand, as shown in Illustration 14. For guidance in replacing the cutting iron, refer to Illustration 15.

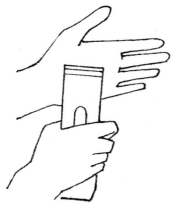

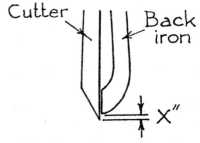

14. *Stropping the cutting iron*

15. *The distance between the edge of the cutting iron of a plane, and the edge of the back iron can be varied. Make "X" about 1/64 in. for thin shavings, and 1/16 in. for thick shavings*

HOW TO MAKE A JOINT WITH GLUE AND SCREWS. A glued and screwed joint can be neat and remarkably permanent.

Let us assume that you wish to join Piece of Wood A to Piece B, and that there is room for only one screw.

First, you should drill in Piece A a hole that is very slightly larger than the shank (or smooth cylindrical part) of the screw. The screw should be an easy running fit in the hole, without being free to slip about.

Then countersink the outer surface at 45° so that the head of the screw will snuggle down neatly into the wood. (Special countersinking tools can be purchased, for use with a wheel brace. They cost only a few pence.)

Then put the two pieces of wood together in the required position, place the screw in the hole you have drilled for it, and use the point of the screw to "spot off" a centre mark on the second piece of wood.

Then separate the two pieces of wood and drill a "lead in" hole at the centre mark you have just made. For this pilot hole use a drill whose diameter is half the diameter of the shank of the screw. The combined lengths of the two holes should be a little less than the total length of the screw they are to accommodate.

Then put a thin film of glue on each of the surfaces to be united, working swiftly so that the glue has no chance to cool, or to lose its adhesive qualities.

To complete the joint, insert the screw in the holes you have made for it, and drive it home. As the underside of the head fits snugly into the recess you have made for it, it should draw the two pieces of wood together and make the joint satisfactorily permanent.

Don't be discouraged by the technical advice given in this chapter—it may make the task of producing a miniature theatre sound very difficult. But a high standard of craftsmanship, while very satisfactory if you can attain it, will not be absolutely essential. Enthusiasm will be more important, coupled with a certain amount of patience, inventiveness, and the ability to see how unwanted materials and discarded oddments can be incorporated in the structure of your model to add richness and variety to it. Even a humble cardboard shoebox can become an exciting miniature theatre in the hands of an ingenious model-maker.

3

The Stage and its Surrounds

Now you can get down to the exciting task of marking out the main components of your theatre. If you work to the measurements suggested in this chapter you will finish with a medium-sized model that will sit comfortably on an ordinary domestic table top.

These dimensions are not unalterable, though. If you prefer you can make, by halving all the measurements here recommended, a midget-scale model that will be most conveniently portable, and can be packed away in an attaché case.

By doubling all the measurements you can make a really large model, for which you can build elaborate settings, with complex lighting systems. You can people a "giant miniature theatre" of this kind with small puppet-like figures, but you will not find it easy to move about.

The famous model theatres marketed by Benjamin Pollock of Hoxton in the nineteenth century were designed with a standard size proscenium opening— 18 in. wide, 13 in. high. To produce a theatre to this scale, you will have to do a little multiplication, but the sums should not be difficult. (You can still buy quaint and attractive theatre sheets, if you are interested, from Benjamin Pollock's successors at 44 Monmouth Street, London, WC2.)

THE STAGE FLOOR OR BASE. Use a piece of blockboard 25 in. × 15 in. × 1 in. for the base of your theatre if you want to keep the method of construction as simple as possible. If you don't mind a little extra work to get more satisfactory results, fabricate a base from four pieces of stripwood, thus:

24 in. × 1 in. × ½ in. (two pieces)
15 in. × 1 in. × ½ in. (two pieces)

with a rectangular piece of plywood 25 in. × 15 in. × ¼ in. This will take a little longer to cut out and assemble, but it has one great advantage over a solid base—wires for the stage lighting can be concealed in the space beneath the stage just as they might be in a real theatre.

Mark out the blockboard or plywood very carefully.

Begin by making one of the long edges as straight as you can.

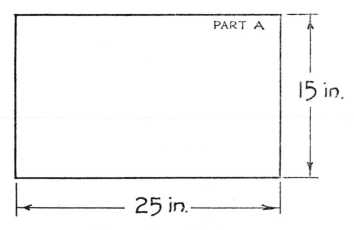

PART A

15 in.

25 in.

16. *The overall size of the base, Part A*

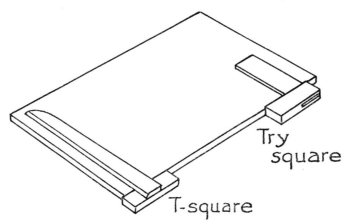

Try
square

T-square

17. *Two ways of making sure that the base, Part A, is exactly rectangular*

Then, using that edge as a "datum" or starting point, mark off with a T-square or try square two perpendicular lines exactly 25 in. apart, as shown in Illustrations 16 and 17. Draw the lines first with a sharp pencil, then scribe along them with a marking knife or penknife (see Illustration 18). Keep your fore-finger on top of the blade, as you do when holding a pen, and use a metal straight-edge for guiding the knife. If you want your work to be especially well finished, draw and scribe all marking-out lines on the reverse side of the wood as well as on the top surface.

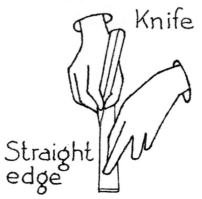

18. *How a marking knife is used*

Then saw along the lines you have drawn, keeping the cut well to the waste side, so that there is a gap of at least $\frac{1}{16}$ in. between the saw-blade and the line. Hold the saw at an acute angle (see Illustration 19). Any saw held at an incorrect angle will tend to tear plywood, though the knife-cuts used for marking will help to minimize this effect.

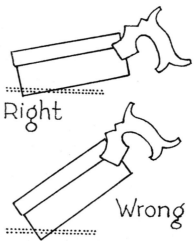

19. *How a saw should be used when plywood is being cut*

Then remove the surplus wood from the waste side of both lines, using a metal plane or jack plane, a file or a Surform tool, or a piece of glasspaper held over a small wooden block. If you use a file, put the board in a vice with a strong thick piece of wood on each side, to support the plywood and to guide the file (Illustration 20).

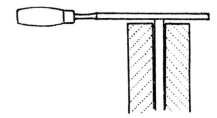

20. *A piece of wood may need support if it is being finished with a file*

When you have finished the two short sides of the base, mark out the remaining side, "rough cut" and finish it in the way just described, and then mark the wood clearly with the words "PART A".

Illustration 21 shows how you can most easily assemble the five component parts of a hollow base. Use a good adhesive, with small countersunk head screws, as described in Chapter 2. Tidy the joints with fine glasspaper when the adhesive has had a chance to dry or set.

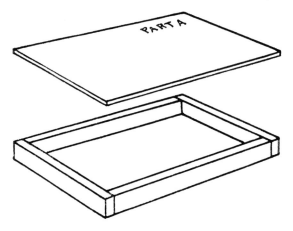

21. *This shows how a "hollow base" is assembled*

The Stage and its Surrounds

Before you leave the base, mark out the top surface with lines that will help you to position correctly the components that are to stand on it. Use a sharp pencil for drawing these lines, with a ruler and a set square or T square. Illustration 22 shows where the lines should be drawn—you will notice that this operation has been shown (to avoid confusion) in two stages, with the first lines to be drawn shown in the upper part of the illustration.

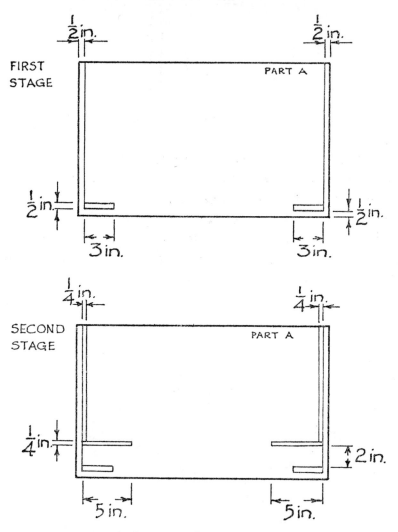

22. *The base is marked out, in two stages*

Then cut two wood locating blocks, each 2 in. × 1¼ in. × ¾ in., and place them on Part A in the positions shown in Illustration 23. Use glue and one countersunk head wood screw, placed centrally, to fix each block to the base. Illustration 24 shows how the base should appear when you have done this.

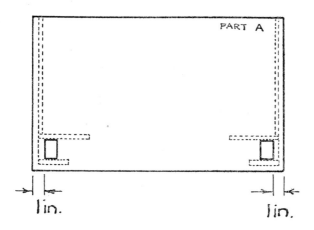

23. *Two wood locating blocks are added to the base*

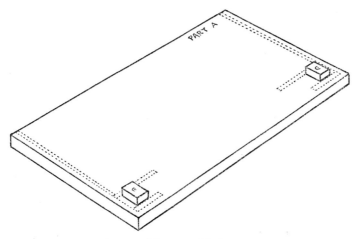

24. *The wood locating blocks in position*

THE PROSCENIUM ARCH. The two largest components of the proscenium arch (Parts B and C) are shown in perspective in Illustration 25. The base is shown in this illustration, too, for clarity. It is drawn with dotted lines.

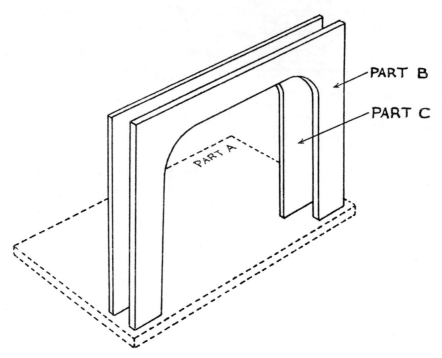

PART B

PART C

PART A

25. *The largest components of the proscenium arch*

Part B is the front surface of the proscenium arch—that is, the side that the audience will see. Use blockboard $\frac{1}{2}$ in. thick for this part, if you can obtain it. This is not so liable to warp as $\frac{1}{4}$ in. plywood, which will, however, be sufficiently rigid for the concealed surface, Part C.

The dimensions suggested for Parts B and C are shown in Illustrations 26 and 27. Of course, you will not be able to cut exactly to the curved contours shown with an ordinary hand saw or tenon saw. Use a bow saw, if you have one. If you haven't, put a large flat piece of wood under the piece of blockboard or plywood you are about to work on, so that you will not damage the table top or working surface underneath, and then drill a number of holes that are almost touching, just outside the required outline. You will find it quite easy, then, to break down the connecting pieces and to slice away the rest of the wood with a sharp chisel. If you have a wooden mallet you can use it to provide the downward pressure.

2. Black makes an excellent background for simple, cut-out stand-up shapes (see Chapter 4)

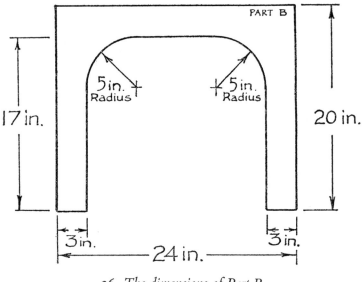

26. *The dimensions of Part B*

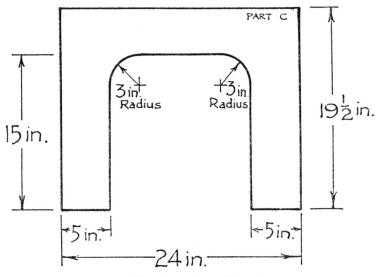

27. *The dimensions of Part C*

Illustration 28 shows where you can drill holes in Part B to take two counter-sunk head wood screws. These will be useful for fixing Part B, eventually, to the locating blocks now in position on the base. Similar holes should be drilled in Part C.

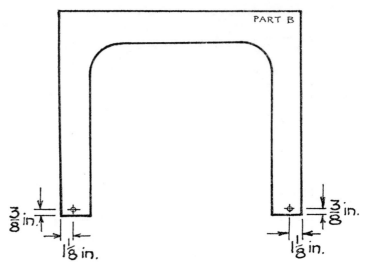

28. *Drill holes for countersunk head wood screws here*

To complete the sides and top of the proscenium arch, you will need three pieces of wood, cut and finished to these dimensions:

PART D: 24 in. × 2 in. × $\frac{1}{2}$ in.

PART E: 19 in. × 2 in. × $\frac{1}{2}$ in.

PART F: 19 in. × 2 in. × $\frac{1}{2}$ in.

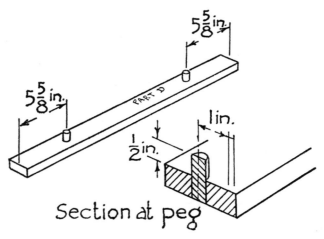

29. *Locating pegs in Part D*

Add two locating pegs to Part D in the positions shown in Illustration 29. Use $\frac{1}{4}$ in. diameter dowel rod for these pegs, or some similar smooth cylindrical pieces of wood. Drill holes in Part D in which the pegs will be an easy push fit, and fix them in position with adhesive.

THE BACK WALL. Part G, which acts as the back wall of the stage, can be made from plywood $\frac{1}{4}$ in. thick. The suggested dimensions are shown in Illustration 30.

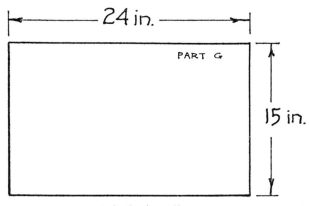

30. *The back wall, Part G*

As soon as you have cut out and finished this part, fix two buttresses to it with glue and countersunk head wood screws in the positions shown in Illustration 31. Each can be made from stripwood to these dimensions:

20$\frac{1}{2}$ in. $\times$ 1$\frac{1}{4}$ in. $\times$ $\frac{1}{2}$ in.

but it is possible to vary the width and thickness to suit any available material.

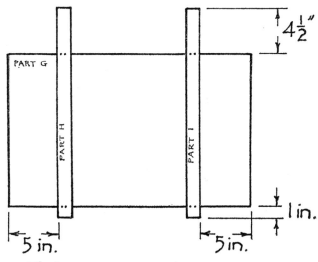

31. *The buttresses, Parts H and I, in position on Part G*

As the lower projections of these buttresses will be used for fixing Part G to the base, drill and countersink two holes in each to suit the wood screws you are going to use. A partial view of one of the projections, with the holes suitably positioned, can be seen in Illustration 32.

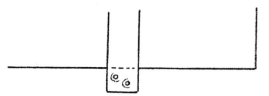

32. Holes for wood screws in Parts H and I

At the upper extremity of each of the buttresses, glue a piece of ⅜ in. × ⅜ in. quadrant, 1¼ in. long ("quadrant" is wood that has been cut to a quarter-circle section). The direction and purpose of these additions can be seen in Illustrations 33 and 34. As soon as the adhesive has set hard, drill a hole ¼ in. diameter in each in the position shown in Illustration 34, and insert a length of ¼ in. diameter dowel to form a locating peg that will pair with the corresponding locating peg in Part D.

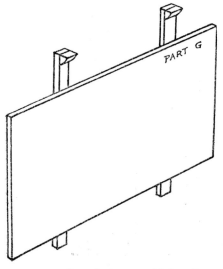

33. Pieces of quadrant are added to Parts H and I

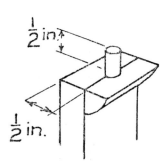

34. Locating pegs are added

36

THE BEAMS. Next, you can prepare the wood beams (Parts J and K) from which the scenery of your theatre will be suspended. Each will be 14½ in. × 1¼ in. × ½ in., and should have two holes drilled in it in the positions shown in Illustration 35. The holes should be just large enough to allow you to slip the beams on and off the locating pegs in Parts D, H and I without difficulty, but without the fit being too sloppy.

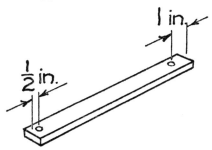

35. Holes to take the locating pegs are drilled in Parts J and K

THE SIDE WALLS. Parts L and M, which act as the side walls of the stage, can be made from plywood ¼ in. thick. The suggested dimensions are shown in Illustration 36.

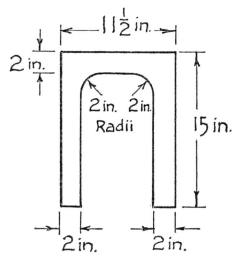

36. The dimensions of Parts L and M

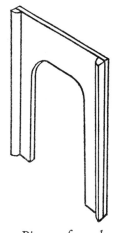

37. Pieces of quadrant are glued to Parts L and M

As soon as you have cut out and finished these parts, glue four pieces of quadrant 15 in. × ⅜ in. × ⅜ in. to the inner surfaces, in the positions shown in Illustration 37.

A PRELIMINARY ASSEMBLY. At this point you may like to assemble all the parts you have been working on, to see how they fit together. The arrangement of the parts is shown in Illustration 38. Don't use any glue at this stage, but use small pieces of Sellotape or some other easily removable adhesive tape to keep the parts in place. You will probably find that a certain amount of trimming and adjustment is necessary, but it will be quite exciting to see your miniature theatre taking its ultimate shape for the first time.

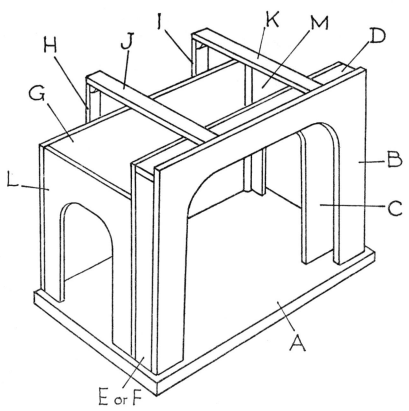

38. *The main parts of the proscenium and stage surround are assembled*

THE STAGE BOXES AND SURROUND. Next, you can make the stage boxes and surround. Good quality white card or mounting board should be sufficiently strong for these, but if you use an absorbent board you will have to remember to use poster colour or some other water-bound paints on it, and not an oil-bound colour or house paint.

The Stage and its Surrounds

In Illustration 39, the suggested sizes for the stage box units (Parts N and O) are shown. Cut out the box openings, shown in the drawing on the left, and then add some guide lines (which will be useful later) as shown in the drawing on the right. Score lightly along the dotted lines with the tip of a knife or scissors blade, and then fold to make two triangular units.

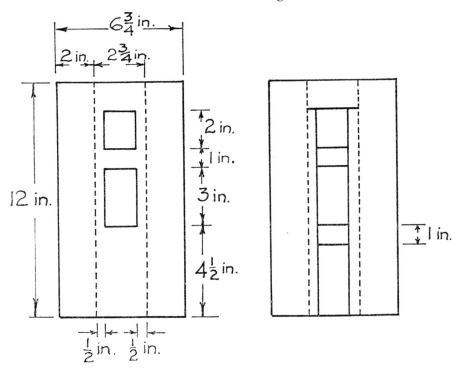

39. *Suggested dimensions for Parts N and O*

Before you give these units their permanent form, though, it would be most convenient to provide the stage boxes with floors and ceilings. Use six triangles of cardboard or strawboard for these, cut to the dimensions shown in Illustration 40. Fix them in position with narrow strips of paper and glue or paste, following the order of assembly shown in Illustrations 41, 42 and 43. Paint or paper the insides of the boxes when you have reached the stage shown in Illustration 42, then seal each of the units up with a strip of paper and glue or paste.

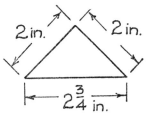

40. *Dimensions of the floors & ceilings of the stage boxes*

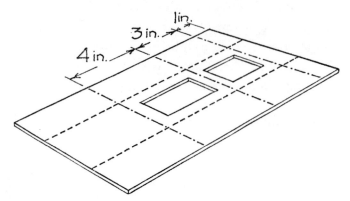

41. *Assembly of the stage box units (1)*

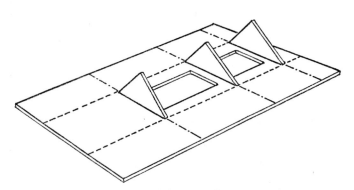

42. *Assembly of the stage box units (2)*

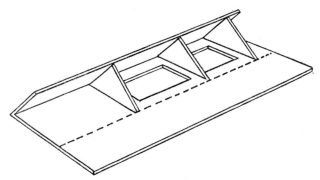

43. *Assembly of the stage box units (3)*

Then draw and cut out Part P (shown in Illustration 44), score along the dotted lines, and seal it up in the same way so that it forms a unit like the one shown on the right of the illustration.

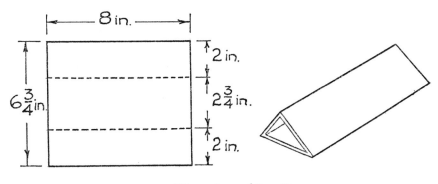

44. *Dimensions of Part P*

Illustration 45 shows the dimensions suggested for Parts Q and R. Use cardboard or strawboard for these parts, and cut them a little oversize, so that you can give them a final trim when you are ready to try them in position.

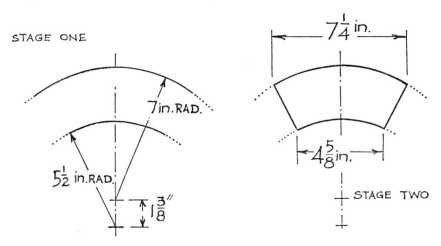

45. *This shows the easiest way to draw Parts Q and R*

Illustration 46 shows how Parts N, O and P are glued, on the final assembly, to Part C. Parts Q and R are used to fill the gaps so that the stage surround has as its base a smooth, continuous surface.

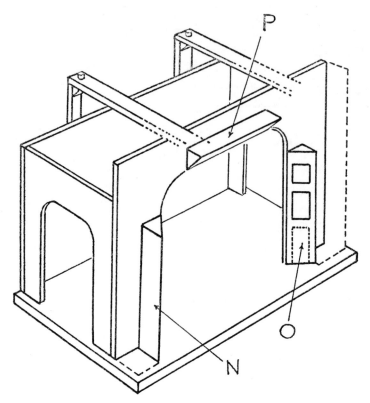

46. Parts N, O and P in position

DECORATING THE PROSCENIUM. You need not make the proscenium of your miniature theatre exactly like the one shown on the cover of this book—if you prefer, you can base your design on any real theatre that pleases you, or you can make a design out of your head. Illustrations 47, 48 and 49 may help you if you decide to work "to the book".

The enrichments on the upper part of the proscenium arch (shown in Illustrations 47 and 48) can be given extra value by being cut out of cardboard or strawboard. This is afterwards glued in position on the plywood façade and, eventually, gilded.

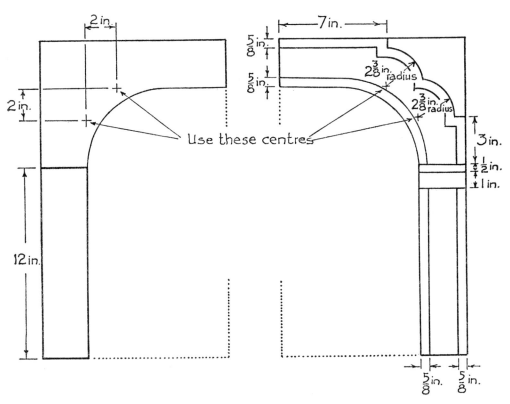

47. *Suggested enrichments for Part B*

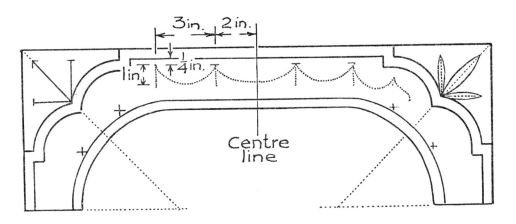

48. *Further possible enrichments for the upper surface of Part B*

43

The pilasters, cornices and other architectural details on the lower surface of the arch (shown in Illustration 49) can be made from small pieces of strip wood, picture moulding, and plywood oddments.

Ionic capitals can be carved from soft wood or cut in profile from cardboard and glued in position.

Bow fronts can be made for the stage boxes from large corks, sliced across.

Curtains and carpets for the stage boxes can be made from any suitable material that will harmonize pleasantly with the main house curtain (see Chapter 4).

With a little thought, you will be able to invent plenty of other refinements.

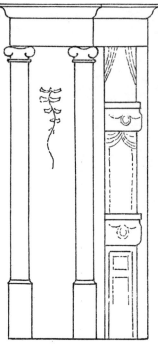

49. *Suggested enrichments for the lower parts of the proscenium arch*

FILLING. When you have finished making out Part B and building these enrichments, make a thorough survey of the fabric of your theatre. Almost certainly you will find a number of small holes, cracks, gaps, depressions, and other surface flaws. Before you start painting, fill these holes and gaps with one of the positive-bond preparations sold at most household stores and decorators' material shops.

Mix the powder with water according to the directions on the packet, and feed the paste into the holes with some suitable implement such as the end of a penknife blade. A useful feeder can be made by shaving down the end of an old paint-brush handle.

Most proprietary fillers are supposed not to shrink as they dry or set, but it is better to leave the made-up surface slightly higher than actually required and to rub back the surplus material with a fine-grade glasspaper after all the moisture has evaporated. When using the glasspaper hold the abrasive sheet round a small block of wood, for convenience.

PAINTING. Choose good quality oilbound paints for the outside of your miniature theatre. Finely ground poster colours can be used, but they tend to become dirty rather quickly if they are often handled.

Before applying any paint, give all the surfaces to be coloured a gentle but thorough rubbing with a very fine grade of glasspaper, known as "flour paper". When using oilbound colours, make sure that you stir the paint properly; go on stirring for some time after the colour appears to have a uniform consistency.

To achieve the best possible results with oilbound colours, apply at least two coats of undercoating before applying the final top coat. Rub each coat lightly with glasspaper when it is dry, before applying the next. The top coat should be laid off with very light brush strokes, each stroke being finished with the tips of the hairs or bristles. This final coat should not be rubbed down.

A theatre without gold or silver paint would seem a very dull place. For these, you can use the metallic colours made specially for model-makers—they are available in small tins and bottles which help to minimize waste. Sometimes these tins and bottles contain so much fluid that it is difficult to get a satisfactory lustre, however thoroughly the mixture is stirred. You may therefore have to drain some of the liquid away with clean blotting-paper before you use the paint.

BRICK PAPER. It may amuse you to cover the rear parts of your miniature theatre with one of the miniature brick papers sold specially for dolls' houses.

For marking and cutting out the paper use a ruler, pencil, set square and a pair of scissors. Each piece of paper should fit exactly on the corresponding piece of wood, but you can leave some edges ⅛ in. or so oversize if they are to be in a position where you can trim them when the adhesive is dry. For trimming, use a steel-backed razor blade or a sharp pair of scissors.

Use any suitable cold water paste or paperhangers' paste for sticking the paper to the wood. With some adhesives it may be advisable to put a thin coat on the surface of the wood as well as on the back of the paper.

To keep the adhesive from spoiling the "good" side of the paper, put each piece face downwards on scrap paper and brush the paste from the centre outwards. The bristles of the brush will then carry the paste safely over the cut edges and will not work it back underneath (Illustration 50).

45

50. When applying paste to paper, work in the direction of the arrows

When the paper is in position on the wood, smooth away any air bubbles with a clean cloth, working again from the centre to the edge of the paper.

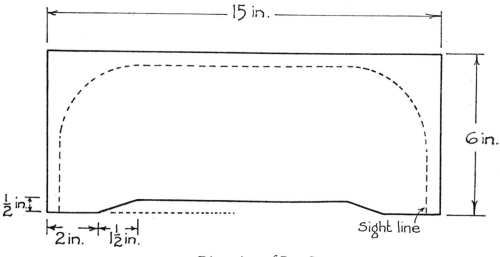

51. Dimensions of Part S

PART S. Part S, shown in Illustration 51, completes the proscenium arch. Cut it from a sheet of stiff card, cover it with the same material as you are going to use for the main house curtain (see Chapter 4) and decorate it with a length of fringe—this can be obtained at almost any draper's—and some applied design, such as the one shown in Illustration 52. If you want your miniature theatre to have a really personal flavour you can incorporate your own monogram in the ornamentation.

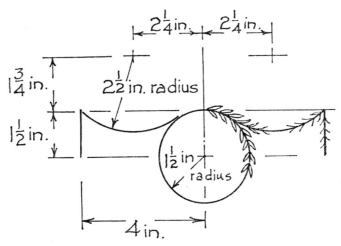

52. *This shows how a decorative motif can be constructed for Part S*

4

Curtains and Draperies

A lot of the mystery and magic would be missing from our visits to the theatre if we could see the stage staff at work arranging the scenery and properties—wearing, perhaps, some most unglamorous overalls or boiler suits. To form a barrier between the auditorium and the backstage regions it is customary to raise and lower an "act curtain", or "house curtain", or to pull a pair of curtains across on a traverse track or traveller if the system has been designed to work that way.

In front of the house curtain—placed, that is, so that it seals completely the proscenium opening—we normally find a steel or asbestos safety curtain which will conform in all respects to the fire regulations of the local authority. Normally, this is seen only once at any performance, when it is lowered rather ponderously to show the members of the audience how secure they are (and, incidentally, to demonstrate that the curtain is still in working order!)

Obviously, a lot of care has to be taken tò see that the house curtain and the safety curtain are pleasant to look at, for they are important features of a theatre and are subjected to close scrutiny. This is how miniature curtains can be made:

THE SAFETY CURTAIN. Cut out a rectangle of stiff strawboard or cardboard, hardboard or plywood 18 in. × 9½ in. and decorate it with some attractive design, or with a selection of advertisements—cut, perhaps, from a well-produced magazine. Attach two lengths of fine string or thread to the upper edge, as shown in Illustration 53, and pass the other ends through two screw eyes placed in convenient positions on the underside of Parts J and K. If you can

3. The enchanted wood in *A Midsummer Night's Dream*. Diagrams that will help you to reproduce this scene in your own miniature theatre are included in Chapter 5

tie the ends of the lines to a weight that is approximately equal to the weight of the curtain, you will be able to control the curtain with the touch of a finger.

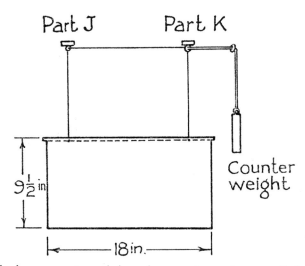

53. *Both the house curtain and the safety curtain can be controlled in this way*

THE HOUSE CURTAIN. This can be made and hung in exactly the same way as the safety curtain, except in one important respect—the house curtain is usually made of, or covered with, some attractive material such as velvet. It can be given extra richness, too, with embroidery, or with the addition of beads, sequins, or lengths of upholsterers' fringe.

TORMENTORS, TEASERS AND RETURNS. The size of the proscenium opening in your miniature theatre can be regulated quite easily by the addition of an adjustable inner proscenium. In a real theatre, an inner proscenium is usually made up of two "tormentors", two "returns", and a "teaser", as shown in Illustration 54. These brief descriptions may help you to understand the function of each:

A *tormentor* is a flat, side curtain, or structure set, usually, at right angles to the proscenium line. It may contain an entrance, or an aperture through which a spotlight can be operated, or both (Illustration 55). Frequently, the prompter is concealed behind a tormentor.

D

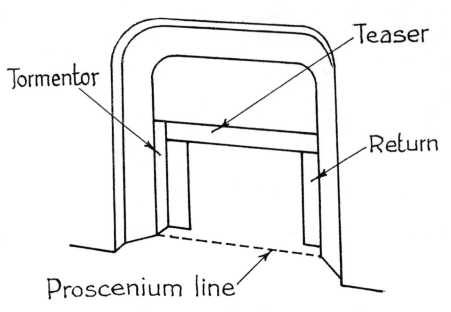

54. *The components for an "inner proscenium"*

A *return* is a flat, side curtain or wing that runs parallel to the proscenium line. By varying the distance between a pair of returns the actual size of a stage opening can be controlled.

A *teaser* is a border used in the inner proscenium that can be raised and lowered as the designer requires.

For the miniature theatre described in these pages a false proscenium made of a teaser 18 in. × 4 in. and two tormentors, each 10 in. × 3 in., will suffice. Use stiff strawboard or cardboard to make these, cover them with some black or neutral material, and "fly" them from some screwed eyes on the underside of Parts J and K, in the way shown in Illustration 56.

55. *How a tormentor is sometimes adapted*

A CURTAIN SET. If you look carefully at the stage of your miniature theatre through the completed proscenium and inner proscenium, it will seem rather bare and bleak. In many real theatres a "curtain set" forms part of the per-

Curtains and Draperies

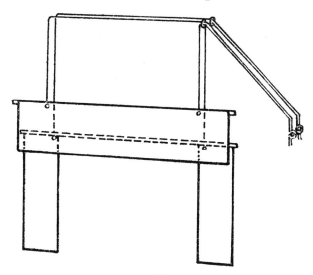

56. How a miniature false proscenium can be set

manent equipment, and you may find it useful to make one for your miniature stage. Use grey or black material, cut to the dimensions shown in Illustration 57. Make stiffening battens from thin strips of wood or rigid wire, attach them to the upper edges of each of the cloths, and then attach threads or fine string for setting purposes.

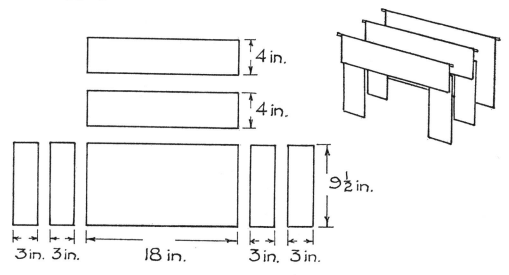

4 in.

4 in.

9½ in.

3 in. 3 in.   18 in.   3 in. 3 in.

57. A miniature "curtain set". The assembly is shown on the right

Curtains and Draperies

The method by which a curtain setting can be "flied" is shown in Illustration 56. A neutral background of this kind provides splendid opportunities for the designer who wishes to make an effective décor for a play or ballet with the simplest possible means—trees, rocks and other free-standing features can be set up to provide scenic interest, and "groundrows" (that is, low flats with cut out silhouettes) can be used to suggest land forms in the middle distance. Illustration 58 shows the kind of setting you can make quite easily if you have taken the trouble to fit up a curtain surround.

58. *An easy way of making "cutout" scenery for use with a curtain set. Each piece of scenery is attached to a matchbox, for stability*

5

How to Build Up a Three-dimensional Scene with Flat Planes

Now that you have created the frame for your picture stage, you will want to design and make some scenery to put in it.

Most theatrical settings are composed of a number of different parts that are put together to make an acceptable whole. A good set should do at least three things:

It should hide the backstage area from the audience (and the stage staff and their equipment and anything else that they are not supposed to see).
It should make a decorative or emotionally stimulating background for the actors.
It should allow the actors to move into the audience's view (and out of it) easily and naturally, so that their exits and entrances do not interrupt the action of the play.

A setting that will do all these things is most easily built up with some stiff flat surfaces (usually known as "flats") and one or more flexible surfaces (usually known as "cloths"). These are found in nearly all theatres that have a proscenium stage, so it is a good thing for the model-maker to have a clear idea of what they are like:

A *flat*. In real life, a flat is usually made by covering a rectangular wooden framework with canvas. For convenience, flats are usually made in standard sizes, and are used in sets, each flat in a set being the same height as all the others, though the widths may vary. You can make flats for a miniature theatre from pieces of cardboard, thin plywood, hardboard, or almost any other thin, rigid material. Sometimes, a flat that is to be used in an "interior" scene will have a door or window incorporated in it. A flat of this kind (Illustration 59) is quite easy to reproduce on a miniature scale.

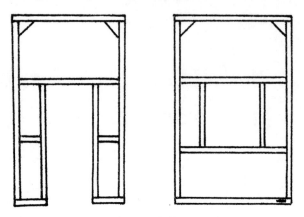

59. *Flats with (a) a door and (b) a window incorporated*

A *cloth*. In real life, a cloth is usually a rectangular sheet of canvas. This is attached to, and hangs from, a straight length of wood called a "batten". Another batten is normally attached to the bottom edge of the cloth, to weight it and keep it taut. Cloths are popular with touring theatrical companies because they can be rolled up and transported quite easily.

On a miniature scale, cloths can be best represented with sheets of paper or cardboard, because these are so easy to draw and paint on. Lengths of stripwood can be attached with glue to the top and bottom of each, to act as miniature battens (Illustration 60).

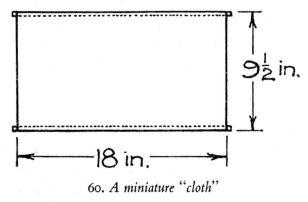

60. *A miniature "cloth"*

How to Build Up a Three-dimensional Scene

TO FLY FLATS AND CLOTHS. In a real theatre, you will easily see a complicated system of beams at a considerable height above the stage. These beams are known as the "grid", and they are fitted with pulleys and ropes that enable scenery and lighting to be suspended out of sight of the audience, or lowered when it is necessary for them to be brought into view. In a miniature theatre, it is not advisable to have a very complicated grid—a number of small screw eyes can be inserted in the undersides of Parts J and K at regular intervals, as shown in Illustration 61, and these can be used as suspension points.

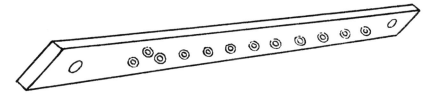

61. *Screw eyes on the underside of Part J. (Part K is fitted similarly)*

To "set" a cloth (that is, to hang it in its correct position) make two small holes in the upper batten, put the end of a length of thread or fine string through each, and secure. Then carry these "lines" through a pair of the screw eyes in the way shown in Illustration 62. A row of screw eyes can be inserted near

Part J   Part K

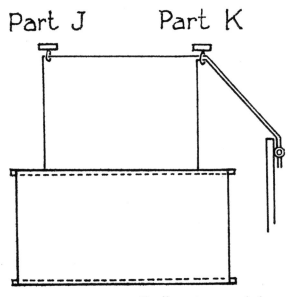

62. *An easy way to "set" a miniature cloth*

the upper outer edge of Part M, and these can be used as "cleats" for securing the stage staff's ends of the lines.

Flats, in a real theatre, may be "set" (or placed in their correct position) in any one of a number of different ways. They may be:

"Flied", in the way just described for cloths.

Fixed to the stage floor with screwed brackets or supported with wooden "braces".

Fastened to adjoining flats with pieces of rope or cord (these are usually known as "lashlines").

Sellotape, gummed strip and similar light fastenings can be used when miniature flats are being assembled on a miniature stage.

WINGS. These are flats that are arranged, in traditional settings, at each side of the acting area, and parallel (or nearly so) to the proscenium line. As a setting that uses wings is quite easy to design and construct, you may like to try making the woodland scene shown in Plate 3. You can assume, if you wish, that this is to be a setting for part of William Shakespeare's *A Midsummer Night's Dream*— —the scene, perhaps, where poor Bottom the Weaver wakes up and finds that he has been magically endowed with an ass's head.

THE BACKDROP. This is the "cloth" that the audience will see at the very back of the acting area. Make it from a piece of stout paper or card 18 in. × 9½ in., and prepare it for setting with miniature battens and lines in the way described in page 55.

Usually, a stage designer will give a lot of thought to the ways in which he (or she) can produce an illusion of distance—it is not easy to make the scenery on a small stage look as if it is part of a great panoramic view, but this can be done if the right tones and colours are chosen for each of the components.

Begin by using only the faintest of outlines, the lightest of tones, and the coolest of colours on the backdrop (Illustration 63). You can vary this design in any way you please, of course, but a glimpse of a distant sea coast, seen through the arching boughs of some leafy trees, can be very satisfying, especially if there is some unusually romantic feature, such as a ruined castle, for the eye to rest on at the furthest extent of its range.

63. *A backdrop for a scene in "A Midsummer Night's Dream"*

THE TREES. In the setting shown in Plate 3, the wings have been painted to suggest the trunks of trees, and extra material has been added, wherever a branch occurs, to break the straight vertical edge of a conventional flat (Illustration 64 shows this).

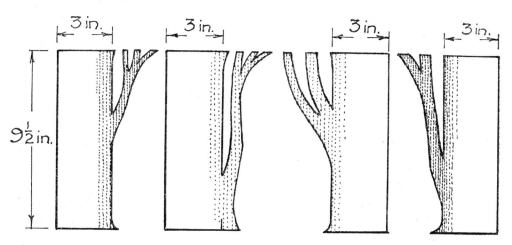

64. *Wings, for a scene in "A Midsummer Night's Dream"*

How to Build Up a Three-dimensional Scene

In order to emphasize the effects of distance, the trunks that are to stand *downstage* (that is, nearest to the audience) have been shaded with darker tones and painted with richer colours than the trunks that are to look as though they are standing in the middle distance.

BORDERS. Borders are cloths or flats arranged in such a way that they appear to provide a "ceiling" to the stage and prevent the audience seeing any lights or pieces of scenery suspended above it.

In the woodland setting shown in Plate 3 the borders have been painted and trimmed so that they resemble foliage (Illustration 65). In each case, the darkness of the shadows and the richness of the colours has been adjusted to suit the distance of the border from the proscenium line—the *downstage* border is stronger and richer than the border nearer to the backdrop, because the former is to act as part of the foreground, the latter is to act as part of the background.

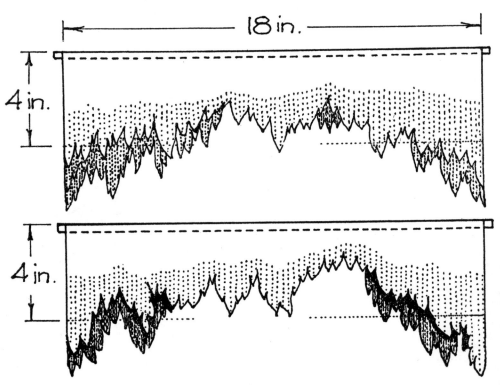

65. Borders, for a scene in "A Midsummer Night's Dream"

58

CUTCLOTHS. Occasionally, you will see a cutcloth substituted for a pair of wings and a border. A cutcloth, as its name implies, is a cloth that has had some part cut away—usually the middle, and as often as not in such a way that an irregular profile is produced (Illustration 66). Cutcloths are especially useful for reproducing natural forms such as rocks and trees and were provided in vast numbers for lavish Victorian pantomimes.

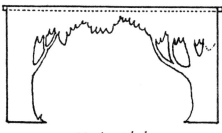

66. *A cutcloth*

6

How to Make an Exciting Scene with More Complex Forms

After you have made a simple setting composed of a backdrop, wings and borders, with, perhaps, a freestanding "property" or two, you will enjoy designing and making a more complicated setting, using some three-dimensional scenery. Modern audiences tend to become bored by traditional settings, endlessly repeated, and extra interest can be aroused by designers who experiment with some of the countless variations on the "box set".

First, let us consider the advantages of raising some part or parts of the stage so that a setting is produced in which the actors and actresses can perform at more than one level. People who are used to seeing the exciting settings created for films and television dramas may find plays performed on a flat platform rather tedious—except, perhaps, in the friendly conditions of a village hall, where all the amateur actors are known personally by all the members of the audience, and a performance is judged by slightly different standards from a professional show.

In the setting described in this chapter, cardboard boxes are used to suggest the movable rostrums now favoured by so many designers who work for the "real" theatre. You can equip yourself for some exciting work on a miniature scale by collecting empty match and cigarette boxes, sweet cartons, and other light and expendable containers. You may even get the initial idea for a first-rate design by combining a few of these, in a haphazard way, on your stage.

Do you know the story of *Oliver Twist*? You probably know how young Oliver, in the parish workhouse, asked for more gruel and by doing so brought upon himself the wrath of Mr. Bumble and the Board of Guardians, but do you remember the rest of his adventures and misadventures—how he was apprenticed to Mr. Sowerberry the undertaker; how, after being cruelly thrashed, he ran away; and how he was found by the Artful Dodger and taken to Mr. Fagin's nest of young thieves? The setting shown in Plate 4 has been designed to suggest the dark and noisome attic in which Fagin gives young Oliver a home, and where the boy is given a few elementary lessons in picking pockets. It will make an effective contrast to the fresh woodland scene described in the last chapter.

To reproduce the setting shown in the plate, you will need, as a start, three cardboard boxes of the dimensions shown in Illustration 67. If you are unable to obtain any boxes that are exactly the right size, you can adapt the setting slightly to suit any boxes that may be available, or you can cut and fold some flat pieces of cardboard to produce solid shapes that will do as well as boxes, as shown in Illustration 68.

Rectangular pieces of cardboard, strawboard or hardboard can be cut out to represent standard flats, as shown in Illustration 69. Dark borders that suggest a crumbling, cobwebby ceiling are shown in Illustration 70.

The window (Illustration 71) can be cut from a piece of thin card. Use an X-Acto knife or steel-backed razor blade to cut away the waste material when you have drawn out the glazing bars. Behind the window, fix an "exterior backing"—a combination of flats or a cloth that shows sky, with the huddled buildings that one would expect to see round the "kip" or hideout of a rogue like Fagin (Illustration 72).

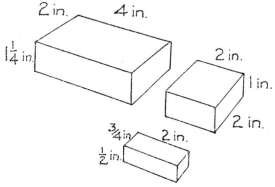

67. *Cardboard boxes with which the stage level may be varied*

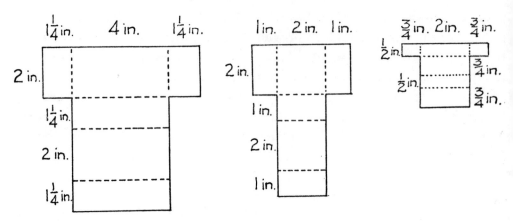

68. *Cardboard can be cut like this, and folded along the dotted lines,*
if no suitable boxes are available

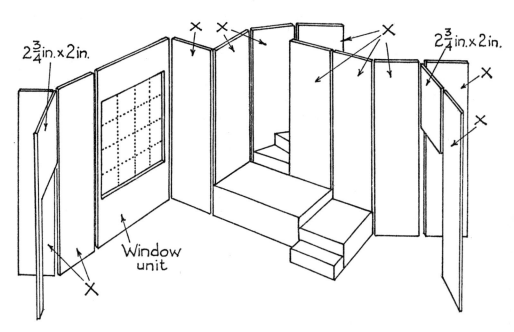

Window
unit

69. *This is how the scene "At Fagin's" can be made.*
All the flats marked X *are 8 in.* × 2 *in.*

13 in.

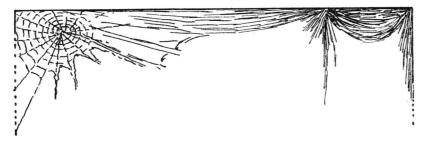

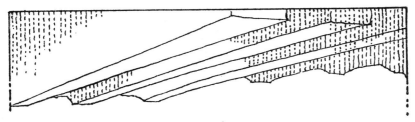

70. *Borders*

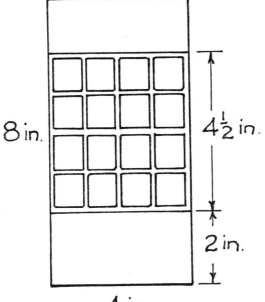

8 in.

4½ in.

2 in.

4 in.

71. *A window*

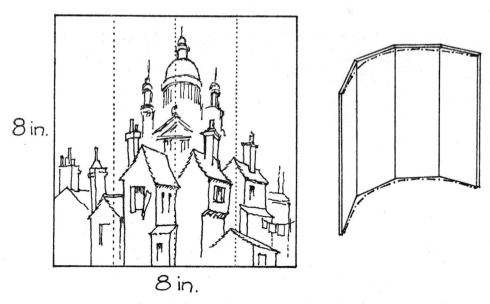

8 in.

8 in.

72. *A view beyond the window. On the right, four 8 in. × 2 in.
flats are used to support this vital part of the setting*

Fagin's stove can be made from a couple of matchboxes (Illustration 73), and the frying-pan that rests on it can be made from the plastic cap used to seal a wine or soft drinks bottle, fitted with a wire or matchstick "handle". You can have a lot of fun designing settings for your miniature stage if you are ready to look around for unwanted oddments that can be converted, with a little ingenuity, into amusing properties.

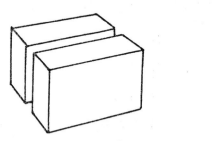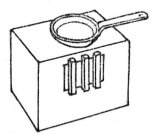

73. *Fagin's stove (the bars are made from matchsticks!)*

4. Fagin's shabby home is a typical example of a "box set". Instructions for making a miniature set of this kind are given in Chapter 6

7

How to Make a Cyclorama for Your Stage

Don't let the word "cyclorama" puzzle you—a cyclorama may be an important part of the backstage equipment of a theatre, but you might fail to notice it altogether unless its uses had been pointed out to you! Briefly, a cyclorama is an expansive and specially contrived surface that forms a neutral background to a picture stage. It may be used for a wide variety of reasons. If used for no other purpose, it may be invaluable for suggesting the sky.

How cycloramas are made. In real theatres, several different kinds of cyclorama are found, the most commonly used being:

A *drapery cyclorama*, or "panorama cloth", made by hanging plain neutral-coloured cloth from a U-shaped or horseshoe-shaped supporting frame.

A *black cyclorama*, made in the same way, with closely woven material that will not shine. Simple but most effective settings can be made by standing small pieces of cut-out scenery in front of a black cyclorama.

A *sky cyclorama*. A sky cyclorama is usually made of tightly stretched duck or linen canvas, painted light blue, and illuminated so that it gives an effect of infinite distance. Unlike a "backdrop", which is quite flat, a true cyclorama is gently curved and is free from folds and wrinkles which would throw undesirable shadows.

A *dome or "horizont"*. This is a permanent, large, concave surface, usually made of concrete or plaster, that takes the place of the backcloth in some theatres as the extreme limit of the spectator's vision. The shape of a full cyclorama is like that of the peel off an orange, quartered (see Illustration 74).

E   65

How to Make a Cyclorama for Your Stage

Clearly, a theatre or a miniature theatre fitted with a full cyclorama will restrict the stage designer considerably—the permanent structure over the stage will make it impossible for scenery to be lifted into the "flies", and it will not be easy to move scenery on to or off the stage by hand, either. This inconvenience explains why full cycloramas, in real theatres, are rare.

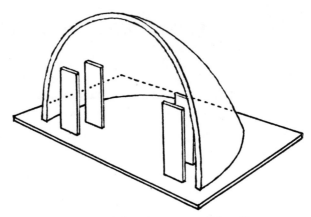

74. *A full cyclorama, or "dome"*

In your miniature theatre, you will find it extremely useful to have a limited cyclorama—that is, a smooth background at the rear of the stage that will provide a suitable surface for lighting effects without interfering with the free movement of scenery.

To make a limited cyclorama that will serve this purpose, take a sheet of strawboard or cardboard that is approximately 24 in. × 12 in., damp it, press it against a large cylindrical vessel (such as a dustbin or clean oildrum) and secure it with string, as shown on the left of Illustration 75. Then apply several "skins" of paper or cloth, using paste or glue to bind them to the back of the board and to each other. When these have been allowed to dry out thoroughly, the binding string can be cut. Then, you can remove the board gently from the surface on which it has been formed. You will find that it retains a gentle curve.

To paint a limited cyclorama of this kind, use white powder tempera colours or poster colour, aiming to produce a surface that is as free from bubbles and brush marks as possible. Then fix it in position with glue or pins, as shown in Illustration 76.

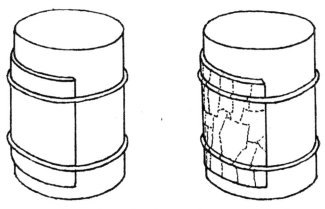

75. *Making a limited cyclorama for a miniature theatre*

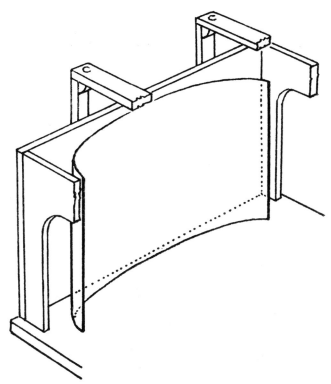

76. *The limited cyclorama in position*

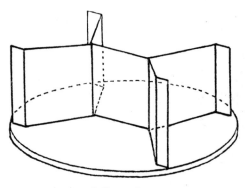

8

A Revolving Stage

A revolving stage is sometimes recommended by theatre designers, since it seems comparatively easy to change the settings on a stage if some part of the floor can be made to turn round. But this type of stage has serious drawbacks that are not easily overcome—and you can by-pass this chapter if you are not particularly interested in instantaneous effects.

Without going into too much detail, it would be correct to say that there are two types of revolving stage. These are:

The *entire revolve*, in which the whole of a setting can be built on one side of a large turntable, another setting being built on the reverse (and hidden) side. Unfortunately, this type of revolve demands a stage with inconveniently large surrounds—this is shown in Illustration 77—and only a few "real" theatres are sufficiently vast to accommodate one.

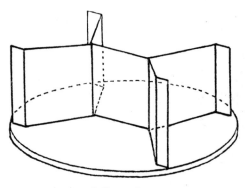

77. A full revolving stage

A Revolving Stage

The partial revolve, in which part of the stage, usually in the centre, turns independently of the rest. A revolve of this kind can be used to turn a small portion of the setting, either in full view of the audience, so that the change is part of the action of the play, or when the curtain has been lowered between scenes.

Should you wish to fit a revolving stage of either kind to your miniature theatre, you will find it easiest to make a "false floor"—that is, a plywood floor that fits over the existing stage surface, Part A. In the false floor, make a circular hole, using a bow saw to make the cut. (If you have no bow saw, you can drill a number of holes near the cut-line, chopping the waste wood away with a chisel, and finishing with a Surform tool, or with a sheet of glasspaper, held round a suitable piece of wood.)

At the centre of the circular "turntable" that is to fit into this recess, drill a hole to accommodate a small length of dowel rod (glue this in position, to prevent it turning or working loose). Drill a hole in the understage in which the dowel can pivot freely, and then drop the turntable into the recess, as shown in Illustration 78.

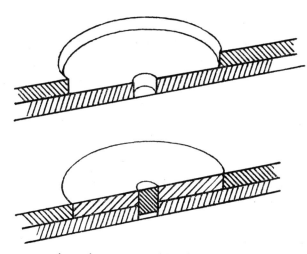

78. *A partial revolve, set in a false floor (sectional views)*

How to Fit Miniature Lights in
Your Miniature Theatre

Theatrical performances are often given very effectively out of doors in broad daylight, but indoor performances usually owe a lot of their especially exciting quality to the powerful artificial lighting brought to bear on the stage and to the people acting on it. Our attention is commanded and our emotions are engaged as soon as the "house lights" start to go down. From that moment until the moment we leave the theatre we will depend on the successful manipulation of the lighting for much of our enjoyment. So, a miniature theatre must have an efficient lighting system if it is not to appear rather colourless and dull. This chapter will help you to add simple lights to your model without too great an outlay. The little stage will come to life as soon as these are in operation.

THE HISTORY OF STAGE LIGHTING. Until electric lighting became generally available, stage lighting was a hazardous business. Until the end of the eighteenth century, most stages were lighted by numbers of candles, held in ornate chandeliers. Some theatres had "floats"—given that name, which still survives, because each float consisted of a wick burning freely in a vessel of oil or tallow. Both systems were thoroughly unsafe and, as a result, theatres were singularly prone to being burned down. The Opera House at Covent Garden (destroyed in 1808), the Drury Lane Theatre (1809), the Olympic Theatre (1849) and the Royal Surrey Theatre (1865) are notable examples.

The first steps towards safer stage lighting were taken when gas lamps were introduced into theatres in 1817. These were a little safer than candles and floats, but they were not sufficiently bright to satisfy the more enterprising

70

managers, some of whom experimented with the effective and brilliant "lime-light", produced by heating rods of lime in an oxy-hydrogen flame. "Seeking the limelight" is a phrase still fairly frequently used today.

Nowadays, with electric light for illumination and efficient chemicals for fireproofing scenery, fires in theatres are fortunately rare.

SHOPPING. Before you go shopping for electrical equipment, you will have to decide how the lights of your miniature theatre are going to be supplied with electricity—from a battery, which will have to be renewed periodically, or from the household mains supply.

Illustration 79 shows how three $1\frac{1}{2}$ volt bulbs can be run in series on a $4\frac{1}{2}$ volt battery. When bulbs are connected in series in this way, the sum of their voltage ratings must equal the battery voltage.

79. Three bulbs run "in series"

The following addition sum should explain this:
$$1\frac{1}{2} + 1\frac{1}{2} + 1\frac{1}{2} = 4\frac{1}{2}$$
A 3 volt bulb in series with a $1\frac{1}{2}$ volt bulb $(3 + 1\frac{1}{2} = 4\frac{1}{2})$ will not necessarily work as well, since the voltages of the bulbs are not the same.

Illustration 80 shows an example of "parallel connection". The bulb holders are wired up in a chain, and the battery is connected across the two sides. In

80. Parallel connection

parallel connection each bulb must be rated at the same voltage as the battery. For example, if a 4½ volt battery is used, each of the bulbs must be 4½ volt.

Illustration 81 shows an alternative method of arranging a parallel connection that is particularly useful when separate sources of light are required at different points in a setting—as, for example, one might be needed to illuminate the roof-top view in the setting "At Fagin's" described in Chapter 6. The same battery and bulbs are used, but each bulb is wired up independently.

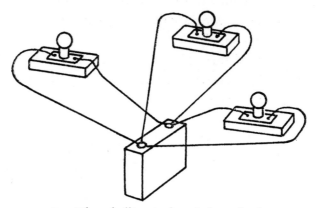

81. *Three bulbs wired up independently*

When bulbs are arranged in series, all can be controlled by a single switch (as in Illustration 82). In the case of parallel connection, any one bulb may be fitted with its own switch, or one switch may be used to control all the bulbs (as in Illustration 83). Illustration 84 shows two bulbs, each with its own switch.

One battery may run several circuits, some in parallel, some in series, each with whatever switching it needs. However, if too many bulbs are connected to one battery this will be exhausted in a comparatively short time. You may prefer, therefore, to use a transformer.

When using a "bell" or similar transformer, connect its main terminals to a power or lighting socket. The output terminals will take the place of the battery. A transformer with an input of 200–250 volt A.C. and an output of 4·5 volt 1·5 amp would be suitable for most miniature theatres.

PLACING THE LIGHTS. No specific instructions will be given for positioning the bulb holders that are to illuminate *your* model theatre, for you will probably

82. *Three bulbs in series, governed by one switch*

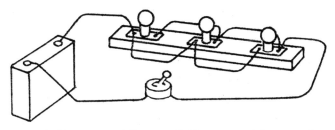

83. *Three bulbs, arranged "in parallel", governed by a single switch*

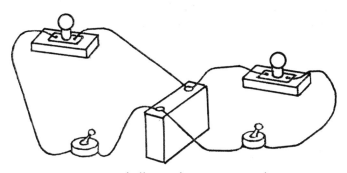

84. *Two bulbs, with separate switches*

enjoy arranging your own lighting layout to conform to your own ideas. You can fix with glue and screws an addition to the front of the stage that will accommodate a small row of footlights (Illustration 85, left), you can arrange a series of battens to hang down from screw eyes in Parts J and K (Illustration 85, right), or you can place lights in the wings, to produce the same effect as portable stage floods produce when they are used in the contemporary theatre.

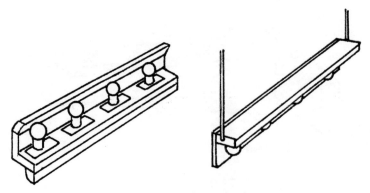

85. *Footlights* (left) *and a batten*

COLOURS. You will enjoy experimenting with colour filters, too—small pieces of coloured gelatine or "Cinemoid" will produce some remarkable effects. The addition of a little blue to the illumination used for the forest scene described in Chapter 5 may suggest that all kinds of strange little creatures are hiding in the shadows, while a deeper blue, used for the scene "At Fagin's", may produce an atmosphere that is both mysterious and sinister. Amber filters can be used for scenes where passionate action would be expected. Red filters will produce some lurid effects, appropriate only for violence and melodramatic stage deaths.

10

Gauzes and Some Other Special Effects

If you have followed the instructions given in the first nine chapters of this book, you should have a miniature theatre that resembles, to a certain extent, the prototype shown in the plates. You will probably have added details and enrichments of your own devising, and your theatre will almost certainly reflect in some respects at least your personal taste. Now, you will be in a position to try out some more ambitious experiments. Here is an assortment of suggestions that you may find stimulating.

GAUZES

A "gauze", in the theatrical sense, is a light cloth that has been woven with a comparatively wide mesh. Lit from the front of the house, a gauze appears to be as opaque as an ordinary theatrical canvas. If the front lights are dimmed and the stage to the rear of the gauze is illuminated, the gauze becomes virtually transparent. These facts are exploited by designers who want to make quick scenic transformations without moving scenery—if a gauze is being used, it is quite easy to obliterate the front or "downstage" area of a setting and to focus the audience's attention on the upstage area simply by throwing a switch. Try hanging a butter-muslin "cloth" an inch or two upstage from the proscenium line and then experiment with different forms of lighting.

ACTORS AND ACTRESSES

If designing and making scenery for your miniature theatre does not give you as much pleasure and excitement as performing plays, you can make miniature "actors and actresses" quite easily. The size of the stage (if you have been work-

75

ing to the dimensions suggested in these pages) will not be sufficient to allow you to manipulate glove puppets or articulated marionettes on strings, but you can cut out some true-to-scale profile figures, like the one shown in Illustration 86, and these will be quite sufficient to add a suggestion of life to an otherwise

Attachment tabs

86. Cardboard characters can be manipulated from the side of the stage, like this

"dead" setting. You can introduce them into the acting area by means of cardboard strips or lengths of stiff wire, which you can control from the sides of the stage. If your fingers are exceptionally nimble, you can fit moving limbs to these figures—jointed, perhaps, with tiny pieces of wire—so that they can make small significant movements at the most exciting moments in the action.

PLAYS

Plays that have been written for the "real" theatre can sometimes be adapted for performance on a miniature stage, or plays can be specially written to suit the resources available. Usually, it is best to screen off the whole area behind the proscenium line so that the stage manager and his assistants and the people providing the "voices" can be completely hidden.

The number of people required to present a play will depend on the extent to which each person is able to change his or her voice at will. Generally speaking, it is best to allot only one main character part for each assistant to read. Then, natural voices can be used as far as possible, and any exaggerations that may be called for—as, for example, the use of extra-gruff or high falsetto tones—will not pall through having to be overdone.

76

Gauzes and Some Other Special Effects

SOUND EFFECTS

You can have a lot of fun arranging some suitable sound effects for your miniature theatre—a sheet of tin or strawboard can be moved quickly backwards and forwards to produce a sound that approximates to thunder, lead shot can be dropped on a metal plate to suggest that heavy rain is falling; you will probably be able to think of plenty more. Don't forget that background music as well as incidental sound effects can be recorded on tape and then played back, at the appropriate moment, without further trouble.

Index